All Scripture references taken from the KJV of the Holy Bible, unless otherwise indicated.

Spiritual Discernment: _The Unabridged Guide_ by Dr. Marlene Miles

Freshwater Press 2025

Freshwaterpress9@gmail.com

ISBN: 978-1-967860-33-3

Paperback Version

Table of Contents

Spiritual Discernment
The Unabridged Guide

Freshwater

Part 1 — The Foundation of Discernment

Chapter 1 --Discernment Is a Gift and a Command

Spiritual discernment is a spiritual gift. It is the ability to distinguish between truth and falsehood, in both the natural realm and also in spiritual situations.

To another the working of miracles; to another prophecy; to another discerning of spirits; to another *divers* kinds of tongues; to another the interpretation of tongues. (1 Corinthians 12:10)

The gift of discernment helps believers identify genuine spiritual messages and discern truth from *error* within the church and the wider world. It involves the supernatural ability to identify whether a message, teaching, or action originates from God or from another source, such as a deceptive *spirit*. A key aspect of discernment is comparing spiritual claims with the teachings of the Bible, God's Word.

Discernment is a gift because everyone doesn't have it just as everyone doesn't have all of the Gifts of the Spirit – except Jesus. Jus as trust is earned, respect is both given and earned, discernment is given, **and** it is learned. Christians are encouraged to ask for discernment from the Lord, so you don't walk in ignorance or darkness. But discernment once received from God must be *developed, sharpened, honed.* *Stu*dying the Bible sharpens discernment. Asking for Wisdom, which God will give liberally also walks with discernment. These gifts all come from the Holy Spirit. Thes gifts re given to Believers, not non-believers although there are those who think they can discern big time and they aren't even saved.

In the Bible, the apostle Paul recognized false prophets and false teachings; that was done by spiritual discernment. While at the same time, false prophets and diviners are not using Godly spiritual discernment, but are connected to the second heaven, where the seat of Satan is to get their information. Some of that information is true; some of it is lies. Discernment is needed to know the difference. Discernment is not used to separate which part you should accept from which part you reject, no--, discernment a must to realize where the information is coming from or who is it coming from to decide whether to reject all the information from that source.

The church is able to protect itself from lying, error, and deception by use of discernment. By church we mean the collective members of the Iglesia, the called-out ones. We also mean individuals protect themselves using spiritual discernment as well.

For there shall arise false Christs, and false prophets, and shall shew great signs and wonders; insomuch that, if it were possible, they shall deceive the very elect. (Matthew 24:24)

This worries me because who doesn't want to be among the very elect?

Not all Christians possess this gift equally: While all believers can and should grow in discernment, some individuals have a unique and heightened ability to discern spiritual matters, which is often attributed to this specific gift.

Discernment is not a luxury reserved for prophets, pastors, or "deep" Christians. It is a command given to every believer. The Bible calls us to "test the spirits" (1 John 4:1), to "watch and pray" (Matthew 26:41), and to "be vigilant" (1 Peter 5:8). Discernment is spiritual survival. Without it, believers walk blindly into spiritual traps, form ungodly alliances, and tolerate subtle deceptions that erode their faith.

Surely in vain the net is spread in the sight of any bird. (Proverbs 1:17)

The problem is that without discernment, the net could be spread in front of a person, and he may still walk right into it. It is only avoided when the intended victim can see it, realize it, process that it is a trap, and then choose to avoid it by turning back or walking around it. All that takes discernment from the Holy Spirit if it is a spiritual trap.

The Holy Spirit is our Guide, but He won't force discernment upon us. We must yield, ask for wisdom, and train our spiritual senses. Hebrews 5:14 says that solid food belongs to those who are mature—those who, by reason of use, have their senses exercised to discern both good and evil. Discernment grows with practice, with prayer, and with intentionality. The knowledge of good and evil is quite a different thing than discernment of good and evil. Knowledge means that you have partaken of it, participated in it... maybe even became entangled in it. Like that net – any net will *entangle*.

Chapter 2 -- No Discernment Compared to Understanding

I met a guy with no discernment. It was the most glaringly obvious thing I think I'd ever seen. He seemed to believe in anything. He trusted everybody. He'd eat anywhere. He talked to too many people. He told his personal business all day long. This guy knows the Bible almost cover to cover, but knows the Bible as words or *nuggets* that he has taken from people and possibly without ever judging where those nuggets came from. Deep thinking? I didn't see it.

Now, this person could be captive in his mind, so I am not judging him, but as he started to repeat the same nuggets over and again at assorted points in our conversations, I began to wonder if he was a robot or was programmed. For sure, I did know that **as he is:** 1. He cannot lead me. 2. I will not follow him. 3. He cannot teach. He will only repeat things that he has heard said. 4. He is dangerous to himself especially but also to others whom he tries to lead.

Of course, I had to use the Spirit of Discernment to recognize that he didn't have any.

In all of our getting we should get understanding. Understanding is not a spiritual gift, but it is available to all. Discernment and understanding are both gifts from God, but they serve different purposes in the life of a believer. Knowing how to distinguish between them — and how they complement each other — strengthens both your walk with God and your effectiveness in spiritual matters.

Discernment, as said, is the spiritual perception **of Truth. It is** the supernatural ability to perceive the truth beyond what is seen or heard. It allows you to sense what is of God and what is not — even when facts and appearances suggest otherwise. Discernment is immediate, Spirit-led, and often intuitive.

It enables you to detect motives, spiritual influences, and unseen dangers. Discernment is more about spiritual sensitivity than mental reasoning.

Hebrews 5:14 reminds us that mature believers have their senses trained to discern both good and evil. Discernment is sharpened through practice, prayer, and yielding to the Holy Spirit. But it is evident from that verse that a Christian cannot **mature** in the things of God without discernment.

Understanding is the ability to comprehend and make sense of information, situations, and spiritual truths. It allows you to apply Wisdom, which is the correct use of Knowledge, to what you perceive and make informed decisions based on knowledge and insight. Wisdom is from God while knowledge can be either mundane information from man, or from God as in the spiritual gift of the Word of Knowledge. That "knowledge" is usually false knowledge and it can come from the second heaven as in psychic information. Saved or unsaved we make decisions 24 hours a day, all day, all night. What we decide to do and then actually execute tells the spirit world who we are and who we know ourselves to be.

Wisdom is the principal thing; therefore get wisdom: and with all thy getting get understanding. (Proverbs 4:7)

Understanding involves reflection, study, counsel, and discernment working together to grasp deeper meaning.

Where discernment shows you *what is*, understanding helps you see *why it is* and *what to do about it*. They work together. We should walk so close to both, even with Goodness and Mercy following after us (Psalm 23), we can also say the following:

Say to wisdom, "You are my sister," and to understanding, "You are my relative."
(Proverbs 7:4)

Discernment without understanding can lead to reaction without Wisdom. Understanding without discernment can lead to false conclusions based on incomplete information. When you discern rightly and understand clearly, you move with both spiritual insight and practical wisdom. This balance protects you from deception and empowers you to walk in truth.

Pray for both — and practice both. They are spiritual partners, designed by God to help you live sharp, wise, and free. As we know from the New Testament that in the counsel of **two or three** witnesses every word can be established. Goodness and Mercy + you are three witnesses. Wisdom + Understanding + you are three witnesses. Discernment + Wisdom + you are three witnesses. Do you see how God set us up to be both empowered and blessed?

In the mouth of two or three witnesses shall every word be established. (2 Corinthians 13:1B)

We are surrounded by a great cloud of witnesses. We embrace those witnesses, we do not reject them, unless we are guilty, ungodly and trying to hide.

Wherefore seeing we also are compassed about with so great a cloud of witnesses, let us lay aside every weight, and the sin which doth so easily beset us, and let us run with patience the race that is set before us, (Hebrews 12:1)

Chapter --- Discernment and Discretion

Discernment versus discretion: we must know the **difference.** Discernment and discretion are spiritual companions, but they are not the same. Both are essential for a wise and effective Christian life. Knowing the difference — and when to apply each — can protect you from error and empower you to navigate relationships, opportunities, and spiritual warfare with Wisdom.

Discernment is the ability to perceive the truth — to see beyond the surface and recognize the spiritual reality behind a situation, person, or environment.

Discernment helps you distinguish between good and evil, truth and deception, God's will and the enemy's trap. It is spiritual sensitivity sharpened by the Holy Spirit. Hebrews 5:14 speaks of mature believers who have trained their senses to discern both good and evil.

But strong meat belongeth to them that are of full age, *even* those who by reason of use have their senses exercised to discern both good and evil. (Hebrews 5:14)

Discretion is the Wisdom to know when, how, and if you should speak or act on what you've discerned.

Like a gold ring in a pig's snout is a beautiful woman who shows no discretion. (Proverbs 11:22)

Discretion keeps you from blurting out everything you know or confronting every situation head-on. It helps you navigate sensitive moments with humility, Wisdom, and restraint.

Discernment sees it.

Discretion handles it.

Discernment without discretion leads to recklessness. You may discern correctly but act prematurely or unwisely. Discretion without discernment leads to silence when you should speak, or speaking when you should remain silent. Lack of discretion could lead a person to compromise when you should stand unyielding.

Ironically, in the United States we have both freedom of speech and also the right to remain silent. I want to believe that they got that from God.

Together, discernment and discretion protect your integrity, guard your relationships, and position you to walk in Wisdom and authority.

Pray for both. Live with both. You'll avoid unnecessary battles and stand strong in the ones you're called to fight.

Chapter 3 -- The Open Doors You Didn't Know Were Opened

The enemy doesn't always come through the front door. He knocks everywhere he can knock to see if you will come to the window to see who it is, to see if you'll look on the roof to see if he's coming to bring you a gift—for those who believe in that sort of thing. The Good Shepherd uses the door, but that doesn't mean that there are no other access points for the thief to get in.

One reason a person needs discernment is because the Thief has many disguises and sometimes will use different faces and voices.

The window? Yes, the evil bird that flies to or even bumps into your window every evening at 6pm to make sure you're home. It is unsettling, it may be scary, it is programmed by the dark kingdom, and it is evil. As soon as you come to see what that sound is, it flies away--, it is gone. That was a knock. Now, your reaction to what just happened determines if you open a door, or create some other kind of opening or not. You go into your flesh--, you just created an opening.

A proper reaction to that will cause you to shut that door, close that opening and get rid of that *"knocker,"* no matter what kind of *knocker* it was.

The issue is that as soon as the enemy gets in, he does come to steal, kill, and destroy, but he may come to talk, talk, talk. That may be part of his tactic to get you to not do what you should do, normally would do, or do the very opposite of what is Godly. So we need discernment to know who is talking. Is it an unclean spirit, a familiar spirit? Is it our own flesh? Is it our own soul, such as our emotions? Prayerfully it is the Holy Spirit. If in doubt stop what you are doing when you hear voices (within you) and ask God, is that You? Then also command that all voices that are not the Holy Spirit of God to shut up, be quiet, be muted and dismissed from your spirit, soul, and environment.

The enemy often creeps in through back doors we didn't realize were unlocked—through relationships—some too-good-to-be-true paramour knocking on the doors of your heart and you falling for their hype. If he is too good to be true, he may not be good or true. Yet, he will still knock, or worse, and maybe eventually knocking boots. Still more knocking; too much knocking. Creating agreements. While you think you're making something else—making time, making love, making a lasting relationship? Nope, the devil is knocking, and he is not making anything that looks like, feels like or lasts like love;

he is making hate covenants. Because he hates mankind.

Doors can also be opened by objects, environments, and even seemingly harmless habits. **What you allow, you authorize.** What you ignore, you empower.

Sometimes, it's the "little things" that open the biggest doors: a friendship you knew was spiritually draining, a song that you sing over and over, and may have been singing for ten or twenty years that you dismiss as "just music." While those lyrics are creating your life and you haven't even put it together that you are living the words of that song.

Well, not before, but you are empowered now, *right*?

Money or an object you accepted without questioning what the actual heck is this, and you don't even question its origin.

The enemy thrives on the ignorance and apathy of humans.

Discernment sharpens your awareness to recognize these open doors **before they become strongholds.** This is why Proverbs 4:23 warns, "Above all else, guard your heart, for everything you do flows from it."

In addition to spiritual transference, discernment is attacked day by day. In war doesn't one opponent try to take out the other? Also, in war one opponent tries to take out the other's weapons. Discernment is a weapon, and the devil declared war in Heaven, got kicked out, but kept warring even after he fell to Earth. Or did you think he had stopped?

As a parent, in the natural, you do realize that if the enemy can't get to you, he may try to get to your kid. The devil can't conquer God, but aren't you God's child?

Whether you know it or not, whether you wanted it or not, whether you expect it or are prepared for it, there is warfare, and you are in that warfare. Your opponent, the enemies of God have made you also an opponent. Some of the tactics used against mankind in this warfare are:

- *Lying spirits*
- *Familiar spirits*
- *Monitoring spirits*
- Gaslighting
- Fakes
- Deep fakes.

Warring against you personally. Warring against those around you. warring against your helpers. Warring against your spiritual gifts—hoping you will not even know you have spiritual gifts. But if you do find out that you are spiritually gifted, warring against your using those gifts because using those gifts is why you were put here, it is your ministry, and it will bless others. Warring until he wears you down, if possible. Attrition is a devil tactic.

Tee Enemy will also war against your discernment. It starts at birth. Fairytales, foolishness, lies. All these things make you not believe what you see.

They make a person not believe what they hear. They can make a person not trust their own impressions, feelings, emotions – there is too often someone waiting to control, own, lie to another person for their own reasons.

By tradition, the lies start in childhood lies and fantasies that adults push on children under the guise of imagination. Children are mistaught from the beginning that there is no such thing as witches; there are no witches. There are good witches and bad witches, even their childhood rooms may be decorated with gnomes, fairies, wizards, mermaids, and all kinds of things that are demonic, and the child's little impressionable mind is taught to be delighted at that.

This is right at the beginning, and it is the beginning of distortions that will turn off a child's discernment. A kid may discern that something is spiritually wrong and without the words to say that may just say they are afraid, or there is a monster in their closet. The parent, who really wants to get some sleep may say there are no such things as monsters. Then, what are all the cartoons and kiddie movies about? And now the child doesn't believe that there is anything in the world that may pose a problem to them, spiritually speaking. Basically, the parent has just told the child to turn their discernment off so everyone can get some sleep around here. This is the beginning of making a person spiritually apathetic, spiritually lazy, or totally deceived.

The Word of God says the opposite, it says that we should be vigilant, watch, and pray. Yes, in Christ nothing can harm us, but unless we are in Christ, what shall we do? Pretend?

Of course, not.

Later in the life of an individual, the devil is still warring against a person's discernment. You're not even a kid anymore, so don't help him by getting the discernment knocked out of you by banging your head on the headboard too hard or too many times. Sex, for example, is not a flesh act; it is a spiritual act.

The enemy is a marketplace actor. Saints of God everything you do every day, all day, every night, all night is subject to be on the moneychanger's table; there is a **trade** going on somewhere all the time in the spirit.

The merchandise of gold, and silver, and precious stones, and of pearls, and fine linen, and purple, and silk, and scarlet, and all thyine wood, and all manner vessels of ivory, and all manner vessels of most precious wood, and of brass, and iron, and marble, **13**And cinnamon, and odours, and ointments, and frankincense, and wine, and oil, and fine flour, and wheat, and beasts, and sheep, and horses, and chariots, and slaves, and **souls of men**
(Revelations 18:12-13)

Before we continue in this book, please re-read those above verses: it is a clear picture of what the evil marine kingdom trades in. Jewels, fashion, hair, makeup, perfumes, food, all sorts of finery and items of status, as well as the **souls of**

men. Do you see then how in the world and all day any of those items may be used as tools of trade and deception to the children of men? It's why we really need discernment.

Jesus turned the moneychangers' table over in the synagogue for many reasons, one surely was to keep the bartering for men's souls from occurring in a church which should be a place of sanctuary and safety. People of God, you need discernment to go into a church or "place of worship" these days. You need discernment to know whether to trust the speaker or the leadership. You need discernment every day, all day, and all night. Wear it like your skin--, the largest organ of your body which keeps all kinds of germs, bacteria and viruses from getting into your body 24/7.

Do not let your discernment be stolen. Most often, in spiritual matters it is easiest to steal something spiritual when it is NOT being used. There was a teenage girl who realized that if she acted the air brain, she could attract more boys as boyfriends than if she behaved herself as the intelligent person she was supposed to be. After a year or so of this ridiculous behavior she asked someone, *How do you stop? She actually couldn't stop.* Whatever *spirit* she had allowed in to make her seem helpless, needy, cute, whatever so the egotistical boys, say on the football team could *rescue* her--, she couldn't get rid of it. She had forgotten who she was back when she used her own mind and used Wisdom as well as discernment.

There is an inherent protection built into the things of God or the things from God while it is in use. When it is dormant, well it is simply stored up. In that state, it can rust, rot, or moths can rush in --, it can be consumed or stolen. But when spiritual gifts are being used, the power to use them is being activated and therefore that same power will protect the gift, the person using the gift, as well as the person receiving that gift.

Discernment is not a trophy for the glass case. Break that glass, take out your discernment and use it all day and all night. Yes, even while you are sleeping; it is a spiritual gift, and your spirit man is active 24/7; he can use it even while you are asleep and dreaming.

Ask the Lord God for spiritual discernment. Practice using it. Sharpen it. Win and take your victory laps.

Chapter 4 — Keepsakes, Gifts, and Cursed Objects

Here is one good use of spiritual discernment which is not only is it necessary, it is a good way to hone this gift—by use, of course. Used in the following setting, discernment is a protector.

Not every object in your life is just "*stuff*." Some things carry spiritual weight — for good or for harm. How many people wear certain clothing or jewelry for good luck? They may have a lucky baseball cap or a ring or necklace that they think provides protection for them. While these things have been elevated to a place of idolatry, it still proves that they believe that it is possible that an item can carry spiritual weight, and they think it is to their favor. It is not always to their favor, though.

Throughout Scripture, we see that objects could be consecrated for blessing or devoted to destruction. Joshua 7 tells the story of Achan, who kept forbidden items, and it brought judgment on all of Israel.

The same principle holds today. Keepsakes, heirlooms, gifts, and souvenirs can carry the residue of sin, idolatry, witchcraft, or spiritual bondage. The danger isn't in the item itself — it's in what it represents, how it was used, and the spiritual access it grants the enemy. I cover this extensively in my book which is a great companion to this one, **Keepsakes or Mistakes:** *__Why Some Things Should Not Be Kept.__*

Objects can be subtle carriers of spiritual weight. Objects can serve as spiritual doorways. From cursed artifacts to gifted jewelry, what you bring into your life matters. The Bible gives us clear examples — Achan's sin in Joshua 7, the burning of occult scrolls in Acts 19, and the command in Deuteronomy 7:26 not to bring abominable things into your house.

Discernment helps you evaluate what you possess. It challenges you to ask: Where did this come from? *Who* did this come from? What does it represent? Was it dedicated to God — or to something else?

When in doubt, pray. Ask the Holy Spirit to reveal any object that needs to leave your life. And if you feel a *prompting* from the Holy Spirit, obey quickly. **Freedom often follows letting go**.

Discernment empowers you to examine what you bring into your home, what you wear, and even what you accept from others. It's not superstition; it's spiritual awareness. If the Holy Spirit gives you a check in your spirit about something, don't dismiss it. Your obedience can close doors you didn't even realize were open.

This may sound counterintuitive, but please carefully consider when people want either things you have or things exactly like what you have. It is not always flattery being a sincere form of appreciation. Sometimes people want things that you have or things **like** what you have in order to use as a point of contact, or a representation of you. The person trying to amass those things may be a whole witch or warlock planning to use those items to curse you. Count the items. Perhaps the person doing the asking is part of a coven, maybe even the leader of the coven and they need 12 or 13 things to disperse to their fellow witches so they can work against you.

Saints of God, this happened to me. A person that I knew for many years to have anything to do with the occult came to my house, looked around and then on that same day presented me with a shopping list of things they said they admired or "had never seen anything like that before" that I had in my house, so they wanted items like it. Then they clarified that they wanted the exact item, the exact thing I had. I thought this was beyond weird. But they kept insisting and insisting. I'm a pretty generous person so I told him where I got this that and the other and I could send him the links. No, that's not what he wanted. He insisted that he wanted ME to buy him those things and gift them to him. These were not expensive items, so he, representing himself as a man of God--, I sent him those things. But really, why did he want them?

Using discernment and doing some more sleuthing, I realized that something is not right here. Upon further digging and with help of the Holy Spirit I realized why he wanted replicas of what was in my house. I prayed immediately and also got rid of those things that matched or mirrored the things I had sent or given him

Chapter 5 -- Are They Lying? What's Their Motive?

Most people would most likely use discernment on a daily basis to determine lie from truth. When you hear words being spoken from anyone's mouth, do you not ask yourself, even if silently, Are they speaking truth? After a while you learn that person and what is most likely to come out of their mouth. This is what we call trust--, it is when you no longer need or use discernment to be in conversation or relationship with a person because you now trust them.

This is why you can be so deceived and or so shocked when a person just changes up their "character" and stops being honest and straightforward and starts to be something ungodly and dangerous toward you. This is especially shocking in places where you let down your guard, such as at home or at church, for example.

For it was not an enemy that reproached me; then I could have borne it: neither was it he that hated me that did magnify himself against me; then I would have hid myself from him:

But it was thou, a man mine equal, my guide, and mine acquaintance.

We took sweet counsel together, and walked unto the house of God in company. (Psalm 55:12-14)

Another person I knew used to mock me because I wanted to know peoples' motive or motivation for the things they did and said. He would laugh and try to convince me that something was wrong with me because I was always searching for a motive. In my way of thinking, that informed me as to who the person was. It was not that I distrusted everyone, because I did not. First, I love everyone right away until they prove themselves to be someone that I should not love.

This fellow was trying to get me to turn off my discernment and the method I used to reach discernment, in the Lord. I did not, and he and I ultimately didn't get along, possibly for that reason and other reasons. We didn't get along especially since I found out his real motives for behaving toward me as he did. Saints of God, if a person is not encouraging you in Godliness, what are they doing? Why are they in your life?

But finding out people's motives helped them to be vetted in my eyes, and perhaps determined them not to be a liar, but, instead, a straight shooter, steady and not flakey or changeable from day to day or hour to hour. It was also a way of trying the *spirit* that worked in them.

If they are lying and lie often, most people will distance themselves from that person because lies are destructive and liars are not dependable and cannot be trusted or depended on. That is, if you have discernment. If you don't have discernment or as the Bible mentions, itching ears, you just want to hear something dramatic or juicy. Even if it is an incredible lie it feeds something inside of the person who wants that kind of mayhem in their life or just cannot rightly divide truth from a lie, so they believe anyone and everything. Isn't that the mark of the average child until they get about 5 r 6 years old? Sometimes they start to remember patterns and discern earlier than that.

Try giving a toddler green peas when they hate green peas. Even if you try to gaslight them to convince them it tastes good, they know that green peas are yucky. Eventually that event of you feeding them green peas will not just mark peas as something they don't like, you, the person trying to trick them into eating those things will be labeled as a liar. That child will get a check in their spirit when they see green peas and also you. That is discernment, even at a kiddie level.

As a teen or an adult, how long will it take to know that what you've been told is a lie?

It varies. And, great destruction may occur by the time you find out --, if you ever find out.

Chapter 6 — How to Hear God Clearly — No Confusion, No Counterfeit

The ability to discern is directly tied to your ability to hear God clearly. Jesus said:

"My sheep hear My voice, and I know them, and they follow Me." (John 10:27)

If you want to sharpen your discernment, you must stay tuned to the Shepherd's voice.

Distractions, sin, and spiritual clutter can drown out God's voice in your life. The enemy's goal is to confuse, distract, and distort. But when you live in God's Word, pray consistently, and remain sensitive to the Holy Spirit, His voice becomes unmistakable.

God is always speaking; are you listening? Discernment isn't just about detecting the enemy. It's about staying close enough to the Father that you recognize His voice over every counterfeit. The more you listen to God, the clearer everything else becomes.

You must practice the presence of God. You must avail yourself and practice hearing from God and knowing that it is God. Two good places to do that is right after prayer: be quiet. Just sit or do whatever you are doing very quietly and listen. The voice of God may sound like an impression in your soul. It may "sound" like a feeling.

Now, we must be wise and careful by knowing the other voices that are likely to speak, and we must be sure that those voices are not blabbing in our soul, in our ear, in our lives.

A third way is to always be circumspect. Don't dive headfirst into anything – well any place or situation. I'm not talking about swimming, but an unwise dive into anything may lead to a situation that may be too deep to navigate. The hard part is when it is so hidden or so subtle that you don't even realize that it was a trap until much later and in some cases, much, much later. So just before taking any step, making any changes, or any big decision, stop and ask God. Talk to God, but don't just tell Him what you are going to do; ask Him what His plans for you are. Tell Him what you have in mind and then listen.

In spiritual warfare we can command, decree, declare but that is to evil entities, unclean spirits, devils, demons and that sort of thing. We don't command God, we don't command Jesus, we don't command the Holy Spirit. With any of the Godhead we listen, and we heed and obey. That is, if we are wise.

Chapter 7 — Fake Friends and Fatal Associations

Not every relationship is divinely assigned. Some people are spiritual saboteurs sent to drain your energy, distract your focus, or derail your destiny.

Do not be misled: 'Bad company corrupts good character.' (1 Corinthians 15:33)

Even Jesus discerned who He allowed close to Him it is why on the night He was betrayed he basically said to Judas, something like get on with it, do what it is that you have to do. Judas was the fakest of all fake friends of all times, but his part in our redemption back to the Father was pivotal so it was allowed, of course.

Discernment keeps you from being caught flatfooted. In Jesus' case, He was to be captured and then crucified, but He knew about it and had acquiesced to the Father for our sakes. Thank You, Lord.

Discernment helps you recognize unhealthy alliances, manipulative friendships, and connections that carry spiritual consequences. This is not about suspicion but wisdom. Who you allow into your circle matters. Some friendships will draw you closer to God — others will pull you into compromise. Be prayerful, be wise, and never ignore the Holy Spirit's warning about relationships.

Discernment will keep you from joining in any kind of covenant with a **person** that you should not be in alliance with. People, interpersonal relationships are very dangerous if you get into the wrong one. Recall the Israelites made covenant with the Gibeonites when God told the not to. God will grant discernment, and He will advise you on relationships, but you just have to ask Him.

You join with a witch—it is for the purpose in initiating you to be a witch by spiritual transference. You sleep with a warlock… and so on. Do you think a witch just wants to sleep with another person? No, their chess game is far deeper than that. Sex is means to an end. They may not realize what at first, they just follow instructions.

What instructions?

The instructions from the spirit they listen to. The one that gives them fame, power, money--, whatever they are seeking the dark kingdom for. They listen to the voice that tells them who to next sleep with so they, themselves won't be killed next. And they do it. People of God, this is why many people do heinous things—it is not for the sake of the heinous thing, it is usually something far deeper. They are on assignment to win something, get something, or to save their own life or the life of a loved one that is next threatened to be sacrificed.

Chapter 8 — Secret Societies, Rituals, and Oaths

Secret societies thrive on secrecy, ritual, and hidden oaths—often operating under the radar of spiritual scrutiny. Whether it's Freemasonry, Eastern Star, collegiate secret societies, or so-called harmless orders, the common thread is secrecy and allegiance beyond your faith in Christ.

The Bible warns us against making ungodly covenants and taking oaths.

Let your 'Yes' be 'Yes,' and your 'No,' 'No'; anything beyond this comes from the evil one.(Matthew 5:37)

Secret oaths and allegiance to organizations that compromise your faith can entangle your spirit and hinder your walk with God.

Discernment will help you recognize when a "brotherhood" or "sisterhood" carries spiritual baggage, even if it's wrapped in charity work, networking, or community service.

Discernment will stop before you join in the iniquity of another by covenants of any or many kinds.

Money. Some people seem to lust for money and will do too many things to get it. Some want to borrow. Some want you to give them money; other don't mind stealing from you, even by trickery—they don't care as long as they get the money. Without discernment, they don't even know why. They don't even know they are being used by the devil to provoke you into an ungodly covenant with the demon or demons they have on board.

Shortsightedly, they may think that the end game is the money. It's not. Money is a covenant maker. Money is a contract maker. Money is a representation of a person's life--, their blood, sweat, tears and time. When you hand money to someone you are handing them yourself and yourself as a sacrifice of sorts. You are giving them to put you on the altar or altars that they serve. The end game, at least in the spirit is the **covenant**.

One day my older brother harassed me for $10. I was in college around 22 years old. He was a grown man, married with three children. He was not only not saved, but he was also perhaps one of the most unsaved people, evident by his behavior, his deeds, but certainly not by upbringing. He was very rebellious, but we weren't raised like that. This particular day, he kept asking me for this $10. As serendipity would have it, I only had $10 that day, exactly $10 in cash.

Looking back, who knew that? Who? I didn't broadcast that I'm coming to our parents' house, and I have exactly $10.

So, my answer must be a *familiar* or *monitoring spirit.*

He kept on hounding me and I stood my ground, saying, No repeatedly. Finally, he was exasperated, reached into his own pocket and pulled out about $300 or $400 in cash and said, "I didn't need your money anyway. But if I had gotten it, I never would have given it back."

(Yes, my parents are related to people who behave in this way.) anyhow, looking back that appears to me not a transaction where the person needed the money, but the money was a symbol of some exchange or some kind of tool to create something else completely in the spiritual realm.

I'm not bragging that I used discernment, because I didn't, I only looked at need. I only had $10 and I needed it. However, if he had asked for $10 and I had a hundred, without discernment, I would have put that money right in his hands. Now, whatever he was involved in, spiritually speaking, now I'm a party to it in some way. You don't give just because you have it; you give by guidance of the Holy Spirit and with discernment, Wisdom, understanding, and discretion.

It's hardly any different when your parent or spouse has a perfect credit rating and maybe you're too young to have a credit rating, or too irresponsible or unfortunate to have a good rating, but they put you on one of their accounts to bring your credit reputation up. They don't have to give you a credit card or any privileges on their account, your name just has to go on that account, and you now share in their credit history and credit worthiness. It works the same to the negative in the spirit.

A person who gets money from you takes it to some evil place where they worship – you're in and you didn't even know that you were signing up for anything. Now that your name is on that altar and you don't worship what they worship, the punishments begin. Your life, as you know it, begins to unravel.

By any means necessary? If you don't give so and so this money, they will hate you or stop speaking to you, or leave you.

So?

Guilt trip or not, threats or not, some things aren't worth the price of your soul.

Chapter 9 - Culture and Compromise

Culture is not expected to be a curse, but it can be. God despised whole cities, and more than one, and slated them for destruction in the Bible because of their culture, their lawlessness, their sin. You move to such a place and by collective captivity, you join in their sin, for examples: Sodom and Gomorrah, and Ninevah to name a couple. God had sent Jonah to Ninevah to have that city to repent so they would not be destroyed.

I recall driving into a city some years ago--, I will not name the city, but I despised it right away and still do to this day. Why? I want to believe it was the Holy

Spirit telling me, **No, not here or go home, or be careful** or something.

Maybe it was a haze of sin in the air. It was not a place known for partying or sin, but there was something about that city that immediately repulsed me as I reached the city limits. I had just gotten there but I couldn't wait to get out of it.

It was by discernment that I was able to pick up on the flavor of the place and I didn't like that place. Not only me, but it was by discernment that I knew the Holy Spirit didn't like that city—or, He didn't like it *for me*. Still, I was thinking I'm here now, might as well go to the event or go see the people that I came to see. And, I didn't want to be known as flakey as I had told a girlfriend that I would meet her here and attend the event with her. See the problem here? I compromised on discernment because I didn't want to compromise on a promise a made to a human.

Lord, have Mercy on me!

There didn't seem to be a problem at that time, but it was. A person from that city whom I met at that exact event was a very strong witch who attacked my life, finances and destiny for years until I figured it out. The Holy Spirit was warning me at the time of the inception of this evil even though I wouldn't realize or discern it myself until decades later.

My God of Mercy!

Compromise can be sin. Not the kind of compromise where you meet halfway in a negotiation, but the kind where you compromise your ethics, your faith, your religion, your own spiritual discernment to please another. Every culture on Earth has beauty, history, and value — but also practices, traditions, or beliefs that conflict with the Word of God. Discernment is the key to knowing the difference.

Just because a practice is cultural doesn't make it spiritually safe. Family traditions, cultural customs, or national celebrations can sometimes carry hidden spiritual dangers. Traditions and annual festivals are often the renewal of ancient spiritual covenants from ages ago that we may know nothing about but ignorantly keep renewing every year or every time we participate in them.

Paul warned in Colossians 2:8, "See to it that no one takes you captive through hollow and deceptive philosophy… rather than on Christ."

Discernment helps you honor your heritage without compromising your faith. It enables you to participate in culture without being entangled in its spiritual pitfalls. Culture must bow to the Cross of Jesus Christ, not the other way around.

Speaking of family culture and traditions, there is a fine line between heritage and harm. I've heard too many people say, it's the annual whatever festival and if **I don't go home, I'll never hear the end of it.**

Culture is a gift from God, but not every cultural practice honors Him. Ancestral worship, ritual dances, festivals, and certain traditional ceremonies may seem harmless on the surface but carry deep spiritual implications.

Just because something is "cultural" doesn't mean it's spiritually safe. Discernment equips you to honor your heritage while refusing to participate in traditions that conflict with your faith.

Love your people. Celebrate your history. But never compromise your spiritual integrity for cultural acceptance.

Chapter 10 —Environments That Invite the Enemy

Atmospheres matter. Some places carry spiritual weight because of what happens there — whether it's a home, a business, a club, or a cultural site. The presence of sin, occult activity, or spiritual darkness in a place can affect your spirit.

In Acts 16:16, in the marketplace, Paul encountered a slave girl possessed by a *spirit of divination*. Certain environments attract certain *spirits*. If you find yourself constantly drained, oppressed, or unsettled in a place, don't ignore it. Discernment is your safeguard.

The Holy Spirit may prompt you to leave, pray over the place, or avoid it altogether. Not every atmosphere is fit for a believer. And not every environment should be part of your regular routine.

I may have mentioned in another book, my experience at the 911 memorial site even after the memorial to it was built up. People describe memorials as sobering, but they can harbor much more, especially when it is the actual site of the loss, death, murder, trauma, or disaster. If you are a sensitive soul or you can feel it in your *feeler*, if you can discern it, ask further if you should go there. Ask if you should linger there? Ask if you should participate in any way there? This is not to disrespect anyone who lost their life there, but places of trauma are successful places and open portals to the demonic.

Chapter 11 — When Good Works Hide Dark Roots

Not everything that appears good is godly. The enemy often uses good works, charity, or public service to mask ungodly roots. Paul warned in 2 Corinthians 11:14 that Satan himself masquerades as an angel of light.

And no marvel; for Satan himself is transformed into an angel of light. (2 Corinthians 11:14)

I've met more than one of those in my life and if you think about it, you may have as well.

The first one was when I was in college working in a restaurant. A fellow came in with a date and he just looked all wrong to me, and I felt that he looked at me and looked at me all wrong, so I went to hide so he wouldn't be seated in my section. That didn't work, the manager came and got me, said two people are waiting in your section. I served them and it became a disaster to my life for several years after meeting them--, mostly him.

By discernment I had the good sense to go hide, although no real Christian should be hiding from devils, demons, or evil human agents.

The next one I've mentioned several times in this book already and even wrote another book called: **Blindsided: *Has the Old Man Bewitched You?*** If you want to know more about it, read that book.

The third one--, yes still another – I met in a church. The fourth one, on a Christian website. And yet another one in another church many years later.

Wardrobe and makeup seem to be open all the time in the dark kingdom— same devil, different disguises. We must always be using discernment to successfully navigate this life.

Just because an organization does good in the community doesn't mean it's spiritually clean. Secret societies, compromised ministries, and even occult organizations often use philanthropy and social causes as a cover for darker agendas. This is why discernment is critical. That organization could actually be calling itself a church.

We must look beyond the surface and ask the Holy Spirit for insight. Are the roots of this work pure? Does this alliance glorify God? What spirit is truly operating behind the scenes? Discernment helps you separate genuine Kingdom work from cleverly disguised deception.

Charities, fraternities, sororities, and community causes may also be harboring hidden agendas. Not every good work is God's work. The enemy often uses community causes, activism, or charity efforts to mask deeper spiritual compromise. Some organizations push hidden agendas under the cover of social justice or philanthropy.

Paul warns in 2 Corinthians 11:14, "For Satan himself masquerades as an angel of light." Before attaching your name, time, or resources to any cause, pray. Seek God's heart. Ask the Holy Spirit if the root is righteous.

Discernment keeps you from partnering with organizations or causes that stand against the very faith you profess. Do good — but do it God's way, with eyes wide open.

Chapter 13 —Marketplace, the Mall, and the Hidden Transaction

The marketplace has always been more than a place of trade. In biblical times, it was where cultures mixed, goods exchanged hands, and spiritual encounters happened — for good or for evil. Paul encountered a demon-possessed slave girl in the marketplace (Acts 16:16) she was speaking Truth but it was only by discernment that Paul realized that she was a diviner who got information from the second heaven. That information was not to be spread abroad being associated with his name. So, Paul cast that devil (familiar spirit) out of her.

Jesus drove out the moneychangers, the merchants who defiled the temple courts (Matthew 21:12-13). Didn't they look just like businessmen? Didn't Jesus call businessmen to be His Disciples? So it was by discernment that the motives and hearts of the men in the synagogue were known, and they had to removed from a holy place, the Synagogue.

Today, malls, markets, and tourist shops are no different. Most think when they are using money it is only a surface transaction. It is a physical transaction, but there is another transaction happening in the spirit at the same time. Spiritual transactions still happen, often unnoticed. Items created for idolatry, occult practices, or ancestral rituals can pass from one hand to another with no disclosure and no awareness of the person who is being initiated or victimized. What seems like a harmless souvenir, or a trendy accessory may carry spiritual baggage.

Discernment guards you from buying, accepting, or bringing home things that don't belong in your life. Just because it's fashionable, traditional, or popular doesn't mean it's spiritually clean. The Holy Spirit can alert you to unseen dangers — if you're listening.

Chapter 14 — What To Do When You Don't Know What to Do

There will be times when you don't have immediate clarity. That doesn't mean God is silent. It means He's teaching you to wait, listen, and trust. He may be testing you because He already taught you this and this is your test for a spiritual promotion or upgrade. I certainly met many "angels of light" and it seems that I kept meeting them because I obviously, looking back, was failing the test.

Lord help!

Discernment is often sharpened in the waiting room of prayer and patience. It is sharpened in the Word of God; we must study to show ourselves approved. It is further sharpened by practicing the presence and learning the Voice of God. Does God talk like this? Would God ever say anything like what I just heard? Did God ever say anything like this to anyone in the Bible? Although the Lord can always do a new thing, look for precedence in the Word.

When you don't know what to do, ask. Seek counsel from the Word, lean into prayer, and give the Holy Spirit room to speak.

Don't rush decisions. Don't move in fear. Don't guess in the dark when God offers you light. The posture of a discerning believer is one of humility, patience, and absolute dependence on the leading of the Holy Spirit. When you don't know — stay still until God says, *Go.*

Part 2 — The Open Doors We Overlook

Chapter 15 — When Relationships Become Gateways

A little leaven leavens the whole lump. (1 Corinthians 5:6)

Relationships are one of the enemy's favorite access points. A wrong connection can introduce spiritual warfare you were never meant to fight. Sometimes the wrong person in your circle not only came through the open door you've been praying against and also comes into your life to open it further or keep it propped open.

People come into your life for a reason, a season, or a lifetime, but not everyone comes from God. Some are sent by the enemy to drain your strength, challenge your convictions, or weaken your walk with Christ. Discernment helps you recognize the difference between a divine connection and a demonic assignment.

Do not be unequally yoked with unbelievers" (2 Corinthians 6:14).

This doesn't only apply to marriage — it applies to friendships, partnerships, and alliances. If someone consistently pulls you away from God, compromises your peace, or introduces spiritual confusion, it's time to reevaluate that connection. That's now, as an adult, but doesn't the above perfectly describe what we talked about regarding make-believe, and fairytales our parents taught us and possibly saturated us in as kids? As a child, how would you know that these people who were trying to entertain you were messing you up spiritually? They didn't do it on purpose--, no it is tradition. It is culture. It is what was done to them when they were kids.

Now that you're older, the taunts are different. They may sound a little like this:

Come on, let's go to the bar and you know you don't drink or have stopped drinking—

- Smoke this---
- Let's go pick up some dates---

…and any other suggestions that lead to mischief, crimes or sin.

Or, if you notice that someone is in your life as a taker and a taker only and it is not your infant child that is not a good relationship although we should cherish people for who they are and not what they can do for us. But if you find you are doing all the giving, that's a sign that they are not from God. If someone is in your life, associating with you as if you're in a relationship but they supply ZERO of your needs, emotional spiritual, financial or other needs, yet you are fulfilling some or all of their needs, that is an unequal yoke.

Give yourself permission to Discern, fully discern and listen closely to the Holy Spirit.

Chapter 16 — Agreements: Contracts, Covenants, and Compromises

Sometimes the most dangerous open doors are the ones we sign with our own hand. Agreements, whether formal contracts or casual promises, can become spiritual snares.

It is better not to make a vow than to make one and not fulfill it. (Ecclesiastes 5:5)

When you agree to something that contradicts God's Word or binds you in an ungodly partnership, you risk stepping outside of His will. Business deals, partnerships, or personal covenants require prayerful discernment. What you commit to can either bless you or bind you.

Before you sign, pledge, or promise — pray. Agreements should never be made lightly. Ask the Lord to reveal hidden traps or unseen consequences. Better to walk away than to walk into bondage.

Sometimes we are signing when we don't' realize that we are signing. Sometimes we can sign with blood never cutting that covenant finger. We have blood in our living bodies, yes, but there are other fluids that represent us, contain our DNA and giving away those fluids are equally binding and dangerous.

Chapter 17 — Habits: The Subtle Patterns That Shape Your Spiritual Life

Above all else, guard your heart, for everything you do flows from it.(Proverbs 4:23)

Habits may seem small, but they carry the power to shape your spiritual atmosphere. What you repeatedly do either strengthens your spirit or weakens it. Unchecked habits — gossip, entertainment choices, and time spent with the wrong crowd — can become open doors for the enemy.

By evil associations, even with people who *seem* nice, you are placing yourself in a collective. Whatever is permitted for them may also be permitted now for you, especially if you are a dry Christian and are not prayed up. What begins as a harmless indulgence can evolve into a spiritual stronghold. Discernment allows you to evaluate your habits through the lens of the Holy Spirit.

What habits lead you closer to God? What habits subtly pull you away? Be honest, be prayerful, and be willing to surrender anything that jeopardizes your spiritual health.

Part 3 — The Hidden Influences in Culture & Community (Summary)

Not every cultural practice, organization, or cause is spiritually harmless — even if it looks noble on the surface.

Secret societies, fraternities, sororities, and cultural traditions often carry spiritual roots in secrecy, ungodly allegiance, and practices that contradict the Word of God. What many people see as harmless tradition can actually be a gateway for spiritual bondage.

Likewise, community causes and charitable organizations may operate under hidden agendas that conflict with biblical truth. The enemy loves to use good works as a mask for compromise.

Discernment gives you the clarity to examine every alliance, tradition, and cause before you partner with it. As believers, we are called to walk in light, in truth, and in freedom — never in secrecy, compromise, or deception.

Chapter 18 — Secret Societies: The Hidden Brotherhoods

Secret societies have existed throughout history — some in plain sight, others behind closed doors. While they often parade as charitable organizations or networking groups, many carry spiritual roots in secrecy, oath-making, and allegiance that stands contrary to God's Word.

Freemasonry, Eastern Star, collegiate secret orders — each is built on rituals, secrecy, and pledges that bind participants spiritually. Matthew 5:37 warns us, "Let your 'Yes' be 'Yes,' and your 'No,' 'No'; anything beyond this comes from the evil one."

Discernment helps you see past the public image of these organizations and recognize the spiritual implications. God calls us to walk in the light, not in secrecy. What may appear as harmless tradition could be a snare in disguise.

College fraternities and sororities often mirror secret society structures can be spiritual gateways with initiations, rituals, and hidden oaths. While promoted as brotherhoods and sisterhoods for networking or community service, many operate under spiritual systems of control and bondage.

Many young believers get drawn into these organizations seeking connection, not realizing the spiritual doors they've opened. Oaths, chants, and secret rituals can leave lasting spiritual impacts.

Galatians 5:1 reminds us, "It is for freedom that Christ has set us free."

Discernment challenges you to examine every alliance, especially those

rooted in secrecy and unscriptural practices
— even if they wear the disguise of
harmless and **fun** tradition.

Part 4 — Living Sharp: Walking in Daily Discernment

Chapter 19 — Tuning Your Spiritual Senses

Discernment isn't automatic — it's trained. Hebrews 5:14 tells us that mature believers have their senses exercised to discern both good and evil. This means living alert, sensitive, and submitted to the Holy Spirit every day.

You sharpen your spiritual senses by consistently being in God's Word, by prayer, and by allowing the Holy Spirit to correct and lead you. Discernment grows stronger every time you obey His leading, even in the small things.

Stay sharp by staying connected to God. Discernment fades when you neglect your spiritual disciplines. You don't sharpen your sword in battle — you sharpen it before.

Even in seasons of rest, you are still diligent and observing the disciplines of the faith, studying the Word, worshipping, this is honing all of your weapons of war.

God's Word commands us to test everything (1 Thessalonians 5:21).

But test all things carefully [so you can recognize what is good]. Hold firmly to that which is good. (1 Thessalonians 5:21)

God even invites us to prove *Him*, so we know that He wants us to know what and who we are dealing with.

Chapter 20 — Testing the Spirits

First John 4:1 commands us, "Beloved, do not believe every spirit, but test the spirits to see whether they are from God." Everything spiritual isn't automatically holy. Some spirits are deceptive, counterfeit, and manipulative.

You test the spirits by comparing everything to the Word of God, by examining the fruit it produces, and by seeking the confirmation of the Holy Spirit. The enemy can mimic the supernatural — but he can't replicate God's peace, truth, or righteousness.

If it contradicts Scripture, produces confusion, or stirs up fear, it's not of God. Discernment demands that you examine everything — and refuse to be spiritually lazy or gullible.

The sons of Issachar could discern the times.

Man looks on the outward, but God tries the heart of a man. In trying the heart, God is also looking for motive. Therefore, I certainly feel justified in doing the same. Not to judge the person because the Word says judge not, lest ye also be judged. So not to pass judgment, but I look deeper to decide and know what I am to do in a given situation. An offer or a situation could very well be a test for me, and I want to pass the test. Amen.

Saints of God as soon as a crime is committed in the natural don't the investigators, say on Law & Order or in any police department start first by looking for motive? Well, as spiritual crimes are committed by the enemies of God, shouldn't we all care about motive. Isn't motive something we should know before the crime is committed so we can escape as the bird who sees and recognizes or senses that a trap is ahead? By discernment we see which folks can be used by the devil and may be the type to lay a snare before your or dig a pit to capture you. We can't always see it with natural eyes that is why we need to see it with discernment, which is our spiritual eyes and ears that the Lord gives us to protect us.

Chapter -- Grieving, Quenching, and a Seared Conscience: Knowing the Difference

The Holy Spirit is sensitive to our actions, attitudes, and choices. Scripture warns believers not to grieve Him, not to quench His work, and to guard against the danger of developing a seared conscience. Each of these carries distinct meaning and consequence.

Grieving the Holy Spirit (Ephesians 4:30). To grieve the Holy Spirit means to cause sorrow or distress to Him by our sin, disobedience, or hardened hearts. The context of Ephesians 4 speaks of bitterness, rage, slander, unforgiveness, and corrupt communication as examples of what grieves the Spirit. Grieving the Holy Spirit hinders our relationship with God, disrupts His guidance, and dulls our sensitivity to His leading.

Dulled sensitivity to the Holy Spirit can happen by simply ignoring his urgings, warnings, even signs and messages. Dulled sensitivity is when a person willfully decides to do other than what the Holy Spirit has said. Those people who don't go with their "first mind" as my mother used to say usually are ignoring the Holy Spirit. The "first mind" is the Spirit of God, usually. Of course, one may not know until the choice ends up in disaster that they have made the wrong choice and taken the wrong road.

Quenching the Holy Spirit (1 Thessalonians 5:19):

To quench means to extinguish or suppress. Quenching the Holy Spirit happens when we resist His promptings, refuse His correction, or reject His gifts and workings in our lives and in the church. It's like pouring water on a fire God intended to burn in us. Quenching often looks like disobedience to conviction, fear of man, or suppressing the move of the Spirit in worship, prayer, or ministry.

A sure way to quench the Holy Spirit is to turn OFF Holy Spirit notifications in your own spirit and soul. It is to go outside the coverage area. Where is that, you may ask, Isn't the Holy Spirit everywhere?

God does not look on sin. When you decide to sin, God leaves the scene. Instead of guardian angels, one may end up with a guardian demon, if this is done willfully, often, and without repentance. A guardian demon will gladly lie to you and mislead you to derail, steal from, or destroy you.

A Seared Conscience (1 Timothy 4:2):

A seared conscience is the result of repeatedly ignoring

conviction to the point where the heart becomes numb and hardened. Paul warns that false teachers and deceivers operate with consciences "seared as with a hot iron." This is more dangerous than grieving or quenching — it reflects a heart that **no longer feels conviction** at all. A seared conscience lives in sin without remorse, justifies wrong, and resists repentance. This person is at risk of being turned over to a reprobate mind. This person is either now condemned or so close to being condemned. The next step is destruction.

Grieving saddens the Spirit. Quenching silences the Spirit. A seared conscience shuts Him out altogether.

Discernment keeps us sensitive to the Holy Spirit's presence, prompting, and correction. The goal is a heart that remains tender, obedient, and quick to respond — never grieving, quenching, or growing numb to His voice.

The Holy Spirit is in us to save our lives in this war that we are in on Earth.

Chapter – Discernment vs. a *Familiar Spirit*

People who just *know* things can fall into one of two categories. By the Holy Spirit or by some spirit that is not the Holy Spirit. The usual false spiritual actor is a *familiar spirit*. Many people who operate by *familiar spirits* are deceived thinking they have the Holy Spirit. This is Error and that is the intention – that the person will be deceived, manipulated, misled and ultimately fail and end up destroyed.

The strategy for the evil one may not be that straightforward but that is the end goal and the end game. An evil human agent who wants failure to the object of their hatred may just "pray" for failure to their perceived nemesis. Those prayers for evil don't reach God, they reach the second Heaven, where the seat of Satan is. Satan then takes it to a whole other warfare level and sends in everything, every evil *spirit* he can to accomplish what this evil, soulish praying person wants to accomplish. As long as someone is agreeing with the spiritual realm, good or bad, even if the desire is soulish and is desiring evil, it could come to pass, especially if the desired victim is not Christian and is also not prayed up.

People who have *familiar spirits* feel powerful. The are made to feel as if they know things that others don't— sometimes they do, but everything they know is not necessarily true or valuable. *Familiar spirits* in their goal to convince a person to listen to them and rely on them can tell a person the most useless of information. Even people who think they are prophets, and other people may also believe they are prophets of God, may stand and tell you where you live, your father's middle name, your birthday—stuff they could have gotten off Facebook are not declaring what thus says the Lord. They are tricking first the one who hears and then speaks this foolishness and if they can in order to deceive others with their nonsense. are assigned to people who visit witches, warlocks, wizards, astrologers, sorcerers, necromancers, anyone in the occult. *Familiar spirits* could be in family foundations and transfer through the bloodline. So, all the people who are "seers" for example in a bloodline may be witches if their "seeing" is via *familiar spirits*.

Familiar spirits are familiar for two reasons, they travel in family lines, hence family related. Also, they are *familiar* because they've been there through the generations of that family, and they know things because they were there. A file has been amassed on the members of your family, so they just refer to amassed records in the spirit from *monitoring spirits* to answer séance type questions about Uncle Johnny, or whoever you are inquiring about. It is totally demonic. Tarot card readers and the like are using *familiar spirits*. This is as primitive as taking two soup cans and tying a string through them to talk to someone. (Did you do this as a kid?) I am not saying that the devil's method of collecting information on humans for centuries is primitive, no he's got computers and sophisticated methods that we don't know about. But, I am saying that when asking a *familiar spirit* anything, you will not get the Truth nor the wealth of data that the Holy Spirit who is Omnipresent and Omniscient has. A *familiar spirit* is like using two soup cans with a string tied between them as a communication device whereas the Spirit of God is the real thing for Truth, Wisdom, Knowledge and Discernment.

The devil has information, but uses another system because he is not omnipresent, but he has data on human families. The *familiar spirit* is accessing another *familiar spirit* who knows the answer and then it is relayed to the witch, wizard, warlock, astrologer, diviner, and then that information is relayed to you.

Parlor games.

Don't be deceived.

Now by discernment, we have to discern which *spirit* we are talking to and what *spirit* is talking to us when we ask questions in prayer or even when we **don't** ask questions, but information is just offered to us by chatty lying or *familiar spirits*. Unclean and evil *spirits* want to replace the Holy Spirit in a person's life to deceive that man and steal, kill, and destroy.

Chapter 21 — Guarding Your Home, Heart, and Circle

Discernment isn't just personal — it's protective. You are a gatekeeper over your life, your home, your family, and your relationships. Proverbs 4:23 reminds us, "Above all else, guard your heart, for everything you do flows from it."

Guarding your space means setting healthy boundaries, praying over your home, being mindful of who and what you allow close, and refusing to tolerate what grieves the Holy Spirit. It means keeping your spiritual gates — eyes, ears, mouth — in check.

Discernment is your spiritual security system. Use it daily. Stay watchful and prayerful, always led by the Holy Spirit.

Discernment isn't a one-time revelation — it's a daily discipline. It grows stronger through prayer, time in the Word, and consistent obedience to the Holy Spirit.

Part 4 reminded us that spiritual senses must be exercised. You sharpen discernment before the battle, not during it. You test everything — spirits, situations, relationships — against the Word of God and the witness of the Holy Spirit.

As a gatekeeper of your heart, home, and relationships, you have a daily responsibility to guard your space from anything that offends the Spirit of God.

Discernment protects your peace,

preserves your purpose, and positions you to hear God clearly — every day.

Chapter 22 – Protecting Others by Your Spiritual Gift of Discernment

It is by God's Grace that we have sense enough to know when we don't have the Wisdom, knowledge or Discernment at the level we may need to be delivered from enemy traps and snares. That is when we call on others to pray for us or we submit to the elders in the church (in the faith) to help us be delivered and set free.

Your discernment should be so sharp that you can see things that others may miss. The Prophet needs extra sharp discernment. The Apostle needs keen discernment. The Intercessor's discernment is honed. Iron sharpens iron, so we sharpen the countenance of our neighbor as well. We all need discernment. Spiritual gifts are given; they are not coveted and kept just for yourself. This is why sometimes your own discernment may not serve you, but you need the discernment of someone else to see what you cannot see, even in our own life.

You may be going through in your life, but you just can't discern what it is or even why. Someone else could pray for you or with you only once and then know that this is familial, this is generational, this is ancestral. There are three ancient altars mitigating against you, and then by a Word of Knowledge or other gifting tell you exactly how to pray to be set free. They may end up praying for you and you are set free at that moment in time.

This is why in some services the deliverance minister may not know who they are praying for at that moment, but they get a Word or by discernment they may say, something like, when you were a child, so and so in your family went to the shrine to exchange your destiny with your dull cousin or stepsibling. Suddenly you know that you know that it is you. That was by discernment and also by discernment you realize that's me and your spirit man manifests. These are the screams we hear in deliverance services. All of these manifestations are not staged. I know because I have been blessed by online or TV services in the privacy of my own home. No one paid me to be delivered. Hallelujah!

Part 5 — Prayers & Declarations

Chapter 22 — Prayers for Discernment and Protection

Heavenly Father,

Thank You for the gift of the Holy Spirit and the Spirit of Wisdom. Lord, sharpen my discernment.

Father, open my eyes to see, my ears to hear, and my heart to know what is of You — and what is not.

Lord God, expose every hidden snare, every counterfeit opportunity, and every secret agenda.

Father, let me see motive where I need to see it so I can vet those I meet, interact with, or those I give authority over me, in the Name of Jesus.

Lord, strengthen me to obey Your leading quickly.

Lord, surround me with Your hedge of protection and fill my home, my heart, and my life with Your presence.

In Jesus' name, Amen.

Chapter 23 — Declarations for a Discerning Life

- I declare that I have the mind of Christ and the Wisdom of God operating in me. Therefore I am smart, I can know all things, understand all things, and discern all things, in Him, in the Name of Jesus.

- I declare that I walk in spiritual discernment — I am not deceived, distracted, delayed or derailed by the enemy, in the Name of Jesus.

- I declare that every hidden work of darkness is exposed before it reaches my life because I walk with Wisdom, Understanding, Knowledge, Discernment, and Truth, in the Name of Jesus.

- I declare that my heart, my home, and my relationships are guarded by the Holy Spirit, in the Name of Jesus.

- I declare that I walk in the Light, not in confusion, compromise or darkness, in the Name of Jesus.

- I declare that I do not have communion with darkness, and I do not listen to any entity, spirits, or powers from the dark side. I only listen to the Holy Spirit and the Spirits of God that are around His Throne, in the Name of Jesus, Amen.

The Spirit of the Lord will rest on Him,
The spirit of wisdom and
understanding,
The spirit of counsel and strength,
The spirit of knowledge and the fear
of the Lord. (Isaiah 11:2)

Chapter 25-- Final Charge
Stay Sharp, Stay Free

- Before you accept a gift, join a group, or bring something into your home — **pray first.**

- If something causes a check in your spirit — **don't ignore it.**

- Regularly examine your relationships, your habits, and your possessions for open doors.

- Surround yourself with people who value discernment and spiritual integrity.

- Keep your prayer life, Word study, and worship consistent — discernment grows in devotion.

- Always remember: **If in doubt, leave it out.**

Discernment is not just for crisis moments — it's for everyday living.

You are called to walk in discernment — not fear, not confusion, and certainly not compromise. God didn't save you to live naive, blind, or bound. He filled you with His Spirit so you could move through this life with eyes wide open and heart fully yielded.

Discernment is your daily defense and your divine advantage. When you listen, you'll avoid traps. When you obey, you'll walk in peace. And when you stay close to the Holy Spirit, no counterfeit will ever catch you slipping.

So here's your charge: **Stay sharp. Stay surrendered. Stay free.** And never forget — the Spirit of Truth will lead you into all truth… if you let Him.

Now go live discerning.

Dear Reader

Thank you for acquiring and reading this book. Thank you for supporting this ministry.

May the Lord make you keenly aware of your environment, relationships, and the motives of people, especially those who have authority over you, including teachers and prophets. May He give you Discernment, Wisdom and discretion to handle every situation in life so that you, as very elect one of God will not be deceived ever.

In the Name of Jesus, Amen.

Shalom,

Dr. Marlene Miles

Prayerbooks by this author

While most books by this author have prayer points either throughout the book or at the end, there are some books that are only prayers. You just open up the book and pray.

Prayers Against Barrenness: *For Success in Business and Life*

Fruit of the Womb: *Prayers Against Barrenness*

Beauty Curses, *Warfare Prayers Against*
https://a.co/d/5Xlc20M

Courts of Marriage: Prayers for Marriage in the Courts of Heaven *(prayerbook)*
https://a.co/d/cNAdgAq

Courtroom Warfare @ Midnight
(prayerbook) https://a.co/d/5fc7Qdp

Demonic Cobwebs *(prayerbook)*
https://a.co/d/fp9Oa2H

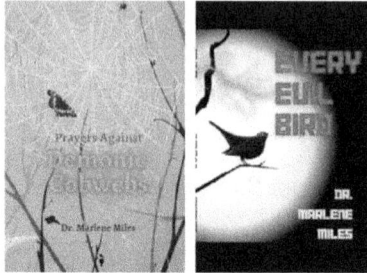

Every Evil Bird https://a.co/d/hF1kh1O

Gates of Thanksgiving

I AM NOT YOUR TARGET: *Warfare Against Haters & the Powers They Employ*

Spirits of Death, Hell & the Grave, Pass Over Me and My House

Throne of Grace: Courtroom Prayer

Warfare Prayer Against Poverty
https://a.co/d/bZ61lYu

Other books by this author

AK: The Adventures of the Agape Kid

Already Married in the Spirit: *Why You May Not Be Married in the Natural*

AMONG SOME THIEVES
https://a.co/d/dkYT4ZV

Ancestral Powers

Anti-Marriage, *The Spirit of*

Backstabbers https://a.co/d/gi8iBxf

Barrenness, *Prayers Against*
https://a.co/d/feUltIs

Battlefield of Marriage, *The*

Beware of the Dog: Prayers Against Dogs in the Dream.

Bless Your Food: *Let the Dining Table be Undefiled*

Blindsided: *Has the Old Man Bewitched You?* https://a.co/d/5O2fLLR

Break Free from Collective Captivity

Broken Spirits & Dry Bones

By Means of a Whorish Father

The Emptiers: *Thieves of Darkness, 1*
https://a.co/d/5I4n5mc

Evil Touch

Failed Assignment

Fantasy Spirit Spouse
https://a.co/d/hW7oYbX

FAT Demons (The): *Breaking Demonic Curses* https://a.co/d/4kP8wV1

The Fold (5-book series)

- The Fold (Book 1)
- Name Your Seed (Book 2)
- The Poor Attitudes of Money (3)
- Do Not Orphan Your Seed (4)
- For the Sake of the Gospel (5)
- My Sowing Journal

Gang Ups: Touch Not God's Anointed

Getting Rid of Evil Spiritual Food

https://a.co/d/i2L3WYQ

got HEALING? Verses for Life

got LOVE? Verses for Life

got HOPE? Verses for Life

got money? https://a.co/d/g2av41N

Here Come the Horns: *Skilled to Destroy*
https://a.co/d/cZiNnkP

Hidden Sins: Hidden Iniquity

https://a.co/d/4MthOwa

How to Dental Assist

How to Dental Assist2: Be Productive, Not Wasteful

How to STOP Being a Blind Witch or Warlock

I AM NOT YOUR TARGET: *Warfare Against Haters and the Powers they Employ*

I Take It Back

Keepsakes or Mistakes

Legacy

Let Me Have A Dollar's Worth
https://a.co/d/h8F8XgE

Level the Playing Field

Living for the NOW of God

Lose My Location
https://a.co/d/crD6mV9

Love Breaks Your Heart

Made Perfect In Love

Mammon https://a.co/d/29yhMG7

Man Safari, *The*

Marriage Ed. Rules of Engagement & Marriage

Made Perfect in Love

Money Hunters: Beware of Those

Money on the Altar https://a.co/d/4EqJ2Nr

Mulberry Tree, *The*
https://a.co/d/9nR9rRb

Motherboard (The) - *Soul Prosperity Series*

Name Your Seed

Occupy: *Until I Return*
https://a.co/d/bZ7ztUy

Plantation Souls

Players Gonna Play

Portals: Shut the Front Door: Prayers to Close Evil Portals.

Power Money: Nine Times the Tithe

https://a.co/d/gRt41gy

The Power to Get Wealth
https://a.co/d/e4ub4Ov

Powers Above

The Robe, Part 1, The Lessons of Joseph

The Robe, Part II, The Lessons of Joseph

Seasons of Grief

Seasons of Waiting

Seasons of War

Second Marriage, Third~~, *Any Marriage*

https://a.co/d/6m6GN4N

Seducing Spirits: Idolatry & Whoredoms

https://a.co/d/4Jq4WEs

Shut the Front Door: *Prayers to Close Portals* https://a.co/d/cH4TWJj

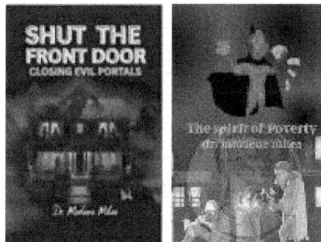

Sift You Like Wheat

Six Men Short: What Has Happened to all the Men?

SLAVE

Soul Prosperity soul prosperity series 3
https://a.co/d/5p8YvCN

Souls Captivity soul prosperity series 2

The Spirit of Anti-Marriage

The Spirit of Poverty
https://a.co/d/abV2o2e

Spiritual Thieves https://a.co/d/eqPPz33

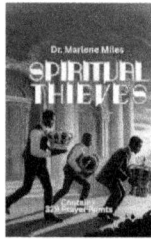

StarStruck- Triangular Power series.

SUNBLOCK- Triangular Power series.

The Swallowers: *Thieves of Darkness*, 3

Take It Back

This Is NOT That: How to Keep Demons
from Coming at You

Time Is of the Essence

Too Many Wives: *Why You Have Lady
Problems*

Tormenting Spirits
https://a.co/d/dAogEJf

Toxic Souls

Triangular Power *(series)*

- Powers Above
- SUNBLOCK
- Do Not Swear by the Moon
- STARSTRUCK

Unbreak My Heart: *Don't Let Me Die*

Uncontested Doom

Unguarded Hours, *The*

Unseen Life, *The* (forthcoming)

Upgrade: How to Get Out of Survival
Mode

- Toxic Souls (Book 2 of series)
- Legacy (Book 3 of series)

The Wasters: *Thieves of Darkness*, Bk 2
https://a.co/d/bUvI9Jo

What Have You to Declare? What Do
You Have With You from Where You've
Been?

When I Was A Child, *I Prayed As a Child*

When the Devourer is Rebuked

https://a.co/d/1HVv8oq

The Wilderness Romance *(series)* This series is about conducting a Godly relationship and marriage with someone who is a Wilderness person. It is about how to recognize it and navigate through it. These books are about how not to get caught up in such.

- *The Social Wilderness*
- *The Sexual Wilderness*
- *The Spiritual Wilderness*

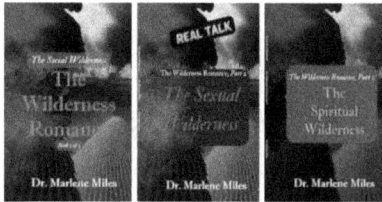

Other Series

The Fold (a series on Godly finances)
https://a.co/d/4hz3unj

Soul Prosperity Series https://a.co/d/bz2M42q

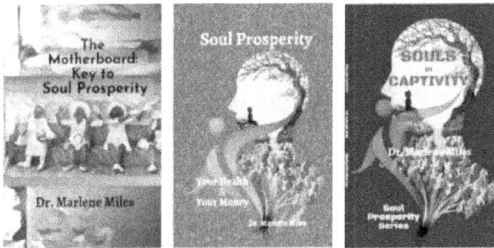

Spirit Spouse books

https://a.co/d/9VehDSo

https://a.co/d/97sKOwm

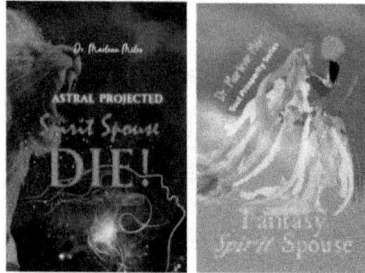

Battlefield of Marriage, The

https://a.co/d/eUDzizO

Players Gonna Play

https://a.co/d/2hzGw3N

Sent Spirit Spouse (can someone send you a spirit spouse? This book is not yet released.)

Matters of the Heart

Made Perfect in Love
https://a.co/d/70MQW3O

Love Breaks Your Heart
https://a.co/d/4KvuQLZ

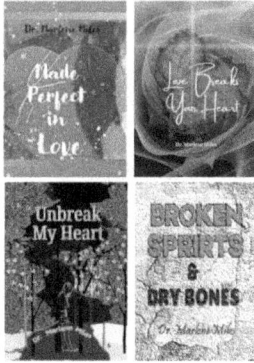

Unbreak My Heart
https://a.co/d/84ceZ6M

Broken Spirits & Dry Bones
https://a.co/d/e6iedNP

Thieves of Darkness series

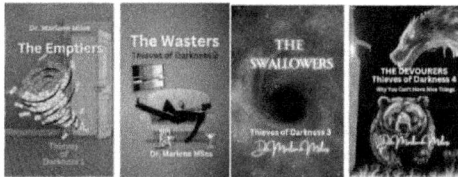

The Emptiers https://a.co/d/heio0dO

The Wasters https://a.co/d/5TG1iNQ

The Swallowers https://a.co/d/1jWhM6G

The Devourers: Why We Can't Have Nice Things https://a.co/d/87Tejbf

Spiritual Thieves

Triangular Powers https://a.co/d/aUCjAWC

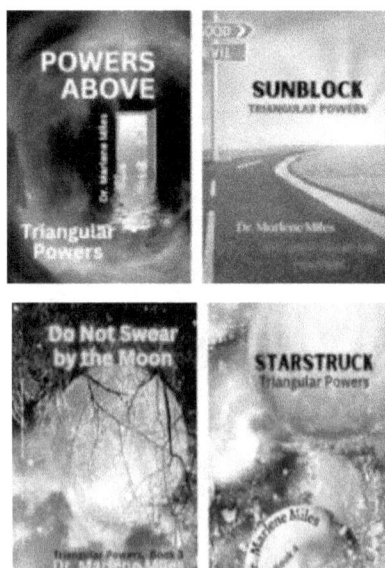

Upgrade (series) *How to Get Out of Survival Mode* https://a.co/d/aTERhX0

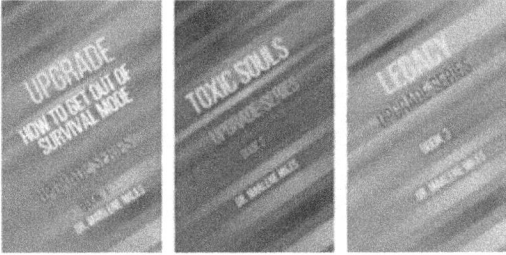

www.ingramcontent.com/pod-product-compliance
Lightning Source LLC
LaVergne TN
LVHW051247080426
835513LV00016B/1794